THE
BLACKPOOL 'STANDARDS

Peter Waller

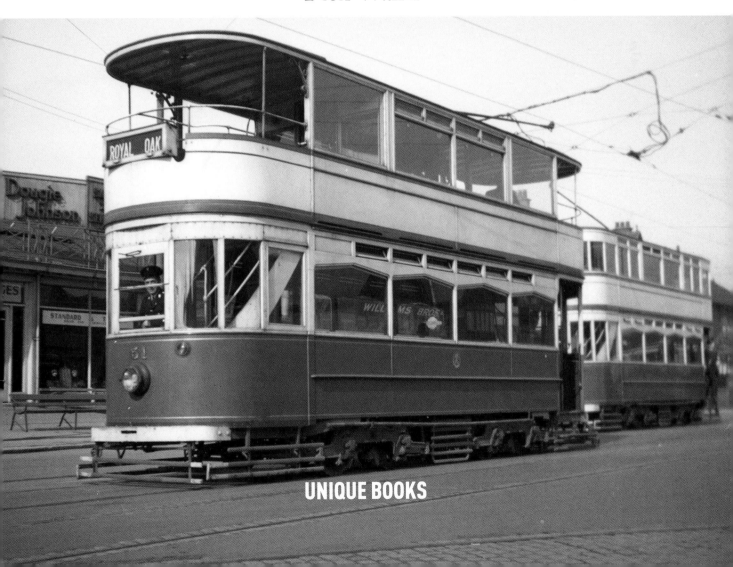

UNIQUE BOOKS

Front cover: A view that epitomises Blackpool: a 'Standard' in front of the Tower. No 40 was destined to become the last open-balcony double-deck tram to operate in Britain; after its withdrawal it was preserved and now forms part of the collection at the National Tramway Museum.
W. G. S. Hyde/Online Transport Archive

Previous page: Examples of the two main types of Blackpool 'Standard' are pictured in front of Marton depot during May 1949. Closest to the camera, retaining an open-balcony body, is No 51 whilst an anonymous fully-enclosed example can be seen in the background. Both trams have been modified with the deeper rocker panel.
Phil Tatt/Online Transport Archive

The Blackpool 'Standards'

Peter Waller

First published in the United Kingdom by Unique Books 2021

© Text: Author 2021
© Photographs: As credited

ISBN: 978 1 913555 06 1

A CIP record for this book is available from the British Library

Unique Books is an imprint of Unique Publishing Services Ltd, 3 Merton Court, The Strand, Brighton Marina Village, Brighton BN2 5XY.

www.uniquebooks.pub

Printed in India

A note on the photographs
The majority of the illustrations in this book have been drawn from the collection of the Online Transport Archive, a UK-registered charity that was set up to accommodate collections put together by transport enthusiasts who wished to see their precious images secured for the long-term. Further information about the archive can be found at: www.onlinetransportarchive.org or email secretary@onlinetransportarchive.org

INTRODUCTION

By THE START of the 1920s Blackpool possessed a tramway network that extended over almost 12 route miles that encompassed both the long route along the sea front from Starr Gate to Fleetwood as well as the compact network that served the town itself. To operate the system the corporation employed almost 130 trams. Many of these, however, were increasingly aged and old fashioned. Thus the corporation needed replacements but the funding for this work was problematic – the slump in the British economy after World War 1 had had dire consequences – and a more creative approach was required.

Traditionally, funding for transport came in two forms: capital and revenue. The former, often borrowed, required sanction whilst the latter, often generated from the actual operation, was generally regarded as funding day-to-day maintenance. New vehicles were generally acquired using the former; however, if the vehicles were deemed to be rebuilds of older trams then it was possible to fund the work through the revenue account and much of the development of the Blackpool 'Standards' was thus a carefully constructed programme funded by the revenue account alongside new trams purchased through approved capital expenditure.

Three older types of double-deck trams were all to play their part in the evolution of the 'Standard'. The first of these were Nos 27-41 – the 'Marton Box Cars' – that dated to 1901 originally; five of these were rebuilt as bogie cars between 1918 and 1923. The next were Nos 42-53 – the 'Motherwells' built by Hurst Nelson in 1901 – that introduced the 'Tudor Arch' design of lower-deck window. The final batch in this trio was represented by Nos 62-68; these were all built by the United Electric Car Co Ltd in 1911 as 'De Luxe' four-wheelers (Nos 62-64; later converted to bogie cars) or bogies (Nos 65-68). These had been delivered with open-balcony top covers from new; the design of these, with the two large central windows, was to influence the design of the 'Standards'.

The prototype of the 'Standards' was No 43; this emerged in 1923 and incorporated a new underframe and lower deck allied to equipment, Hurst Nelson bogies and open-balcony top cover reused from 'Motherwell' No 43. Two further conversions of 'Motherwell' cars – Nos 46 and 53 – followed in early 1923. These three trams were all completed in Blundell Street; contemporaneously with the development of the 'Standard' type came the construction of the new workshops and depot at Rigby Road. It was at Rigby Road that the corporation constructed 32 of the 'Standards'; the remaining seven were all built by Hurst Nelson at Motherwell.

The final four months of 1923 saw the emergence of four new 'Standards'; these were Nos 33, 34, 99 and 100. Like the original three, these were also fitted with Hurst Nelson bogies; all of the 'Standards' fitted with this equipment were subsequently reequipped with Preston McGuire equal-wheel bogies. The first of the type to be equipped with the latter from new was No 142 in 1924.

Four of the Hurst Nelson-built trams – Nos 146-49 – were delivered during 1924; the other three supplied by the company – Nos 150-52 – followed in 1925. The last of the programme was, in theory, corporation-built No 51 of February 1929. However, there were sufficient parts to complete one more – No 177 – which emerged in July 1929. Apart from these last two, all the 'Standards' were constructed with open lower-deck vestibules whilst all had open balconies when delivered. In January 1929 a programme of enclosing the lower-deck vestibules commenced; this work was completed in 1935. In addition 17 were to become fully-enclosed; of these seven – Nos

38, 39, 41, 100, 155, 158 and 159 – were so treated when the lower-deck vestibules were enclosed and the other 10 – Nos 42, 48-50, 143, 147, 149, 150, 160 and 177 – being dealt with some time after the original modification. The last four were completed during 1940.

The 'Standards' were 33ft 10in in length and could accommodate 46 passengers on the upper deck and 32 on the lower. Two types of motor were originally adopted; the majority were fitted with British Thomson-Houston BT265Cs although the BTH GE54 was also used. Eventually all used the former.

The arrival of Walter Luff as general manager allied to the purchase of more than 100 new trams during the 1930s and the conversion of the Layton and Central Drive services in 1936 resulted in the withdrawal of many of the older trams. During World War 2 four of the 'Standards' – Nos 33, 38, 46 and 50 – were withdrawn for various reasons; No 50 succumbed in December 1940 when blown over at the Metropole. Although consideration was given to its conversion into a works car, the damage was so serious that the body was scrapped although one platform vestibule was used subsequently on No 146. A further 18 – Nos 34-37, 39, 43, 54, 47, 51, 53, 142/46/48-50/54/56/57 – were taken out of service between 1945 and 1951; all of these were scrapped by the end of December 1954. A further seven – Nos 99, 100/44/51-53/55 – followed during 1952 as a result of the introduction of the new 'Coronation' class single-deckers whilst Nos 28, 42, 143/45/77 succumbed between 1953 and 1957. This left eight still operational. The majority went for scrap – often after a long period in store – although No 144 was preserved in the USA and No 143 was rebuilt as a works car.

In early 1959 Nos 158 and 159 were modified to become additional illuminated cars. This work resulted in No 40, which had been in store since 1954, being restored to service. However, No 41 was damaged during the year and not repaired.

The conversion of the 'town' routes – Lytham Road and South Pier on 29 October 1961, Marton on 28 October 1962 and the Dickson Road route to North station on 27 October 1963 – resulted in the withdrawal of a number of surplus trams; apart from the first of the streamlined trams from the 1930s to succumb, three of the 'Standards' – No 40, 48 and 49 – were all withdrawn in late 1962. Fortunately all three were preserved – two at Crich and one in the USA.

This left Nos 147/58-60 in service; all four survived until 1966 although No 147 was not used during 1964 it was restored to service the following year to provide cover for two 'Balloons' – Nos 245 and 259 – that had suffered accident damage. As such, Nos 147 and 160 were the last two Blackpool trams in service with swivel-head trolleypoles.

Both Nos 147 and 160 were taken out of service on 11 April 1966 although the former returned to the streets on 19 July. The final 'Standard' operation came on 29 October 1966 when Nos 147 and 159 operated a farewell enthusiasts' tour.

Of these late survivors, No 147 was preserved (again in the USA initially but repatriated to Blackpool in 2002) as was No 159 (at Carlton Colville). No 158 was acquired by the Tramway Museum Society as a source of spare parts and subsequently scrapped whilst No 160 was cannibalised by the corporation for parts for the rebuilt No 143. No 143 – by now renumbered 752 – was withdrawn in June 1990 and was preserved. Returned to Rigby Road in 2013, the tram has subsequently been restored to its original condition with open lower-deck vestibules and balconies.

Thus no fewer than seven of the 'Standards' – Nos 40, 48, 49, 143, 144, 147 and 159 – survive in preservation as does one of the 'Marton Box Cars' – No 31 – which also spent many years in use as a works' car and was restored at Beamish.

Fleet number	New	Enclosed Vestibules	Enclosed Balconies	Withdrawn	Fate
28	9/1927	6/1930***	–	Spring 1951	Scrapped 4/1958
33	9/1923**	8/1930	–	7/1940	Scrapped 8/1940
34	9/1923**	1/1931***	–	9/1947	Scrapped 10/1951
35	10/1927	3/1932	–	Autumn 1952	Scrapped 12/1953
36	7/1925	4/1931	–	Autumn 1952	Scrapped 6/1954
37	10/1927	10/1931	–	Autumn 1952	Scrapped 12/1953
38	11/1926	6/1930***	6/1930	1/1945	Scrapped 10/1951
39	7/1926	4/1930***	4/1930	9/1950	Scrapped 9/1951
40	2/1926	12/1931***	–	1/1963	Preserved at National Tramway Museum
41	3/1925	5/1932	5/1932	7/1960	Scrapped 3/1961
42	5/1926	2/1930***	7/1938	Spring 1953	Scrapped 4/1958
43	1923**	6/1933	–	1951	Scrapped 10/1952
45	1928	3/1935	–	12/1951	Scrapped 2/1954
46	1923**	11/1931***	–	8/1940	Scrapped 9/1940
47	2/1928	4/1932	–	12/1947	Scrapped 10/1951
48	2/1928	9/1931***	2/1938	10/1962	Preserved in the USA
49	10/1926	4/1930***	3/1938	10/1962	Preserved at National Tramway Museum
50	2/1958	12/1934	4/1938	12/1940	Scrapped 12/1940
51	2/1929	From new***	–	Summer 1952	Scrapped 6/1954
53	3/1923**	8/1931	–	1950	Scrapped 10/1952
99	c11/1923**	9/1931	–	9/1952	Scrapped 12/1954
100	c11/1923**	2/1930	2/1930	9/1952	Scrapped 11/1954
142	1924	8/1930***	–	6/1952	Scrapped 8/1952
143	1924	12/1929***	2/1932	10/1957	Converted to works car; subsequently preserved
144	6/1925	2/1930	–	9/1952	Preserved in the USA
145	7/1925	1/1935	–	10/1952	Scrapped 4/1958
146	1924*	1932	–	9/1950	Scrapped 8/1952
147	1924*	6/1933***	5/1940	10/1966	Preserved in Blackpool
148	1924*	3/1931***	–	10/1951	Scrapped 7/1954
149	1924*	4/1932	8/1940	9/1952	Scrapped 10/1954
150	12/1925*	10/1931***	5/1940	Winter 1951	Scrapped 4/1954
151	12/1925*	11/1930***	–	Autumn 1952	Scrapped 10/1954
152	12/1925*	7/1930	–	Autumn 1952	Scrapped 4/1958
153	5/1926	2/1929***	–	Spring 1953	Scrapped 4/1958
154	6/1926	2/1930***	–	12/1950	Scrapped 9/1952
155	8/1926	8/1930***	8/1930	Summer 1952	Scrapped 11/1954
156	5/1927	10/1933***	–	Summer 1952	Scrapped 4/1954
157	6/1927	4/1930	–	12/1949	Scrapped 10/1951
158	6/1927	12/1930***	12/1930	10/1966	Sold to Crich for spares; scrapped 5/1978
159	6/1927	2/1930***	2/1930	10/1966	Preserved at Carlton Colville
160	9/1927	9/1929	3/1940	4/1966	Scrapped 4/1967
177	7/1929	From new***	7/1940	Spring 1952	Scrapped 4/1958

Notes:
* Built by Hurst Nelson of Motherwell
** Originally fitted with Hurst Nelson bogies but later replaced by Preston McGuire equal-wheel bogies
*** Fitted with deeper rocker panels either contemporaneously with the lower-deck vestibules or subsequently

The genesis of the Blackpool 'Standard' type lay in a batch of 15 four-wheel cars – Nos 27-41 – that were built by the Midland Railway Carriage & Wagon Co Ltd and new in 1901. These had been ordered for the newly-opened Marton route. Eventually known as 'Marton Box Cars', all had received replacements for their original Midland-built trucks by 1911 and 12 had received top covers – as illustrated in this view of one of the batch taken in 1920 – between 1911 and 1914.
E. Deane/John Meredith Collection/Online Transport Archive

Between 1917 and 1919 five of the 'Marton Box Cars' – Nos 27 and 29-32 – were rebuilt in Blundell Street Works in order to increase their seating capacity. Each was lengthened and equipped with Hurst Nelson maximum-traction bogies reused from the 1902 batch of Hurst Nelson-built cars, Nos 42-53. With two of the classic – and earlier – 'Dreadnought' cars in the background one of the five – No 29 – is pictured heading northbound at the Tower. The remaining 10 four-wheel cars were all withdrawn by 1927, with the first to succumb – Nos 33 and 34 – being taken out of service in about 1922 when both were converted into works cars.
E. Deane/John Meredith Collection/Online Transport Archive

Of the five rebuilt 'Marton Box Cars' two – Nos 30 and 31 – soon lost their top covers, as evinced by this view of No 30 subsequent to its rebuilding as a bogie car. Both, however, were to regain top covers in 1928. No 31 was, however, not to remain in passenger service for much longer; it was withdrawn in 1934 when it was transferred to the Engineering Department to replace one of the original electric cars of 1885.

E. Deane/John Meredith Collection/Online Transport Archive

Two of the rebuilt 'Marton Box Cars' pose alongside each other. Although the view was taken on the Promenade route, the four remaining rebuilt cars – Nos 27, 29, 30 and 32 – spent much of their career operating latterly on the Layton route; when this was converted to bus operation on 19 October 1936 and with the arrival of the new streamlined cars, the four were withdrawn as surplus to requirements during 1937 and 1938 and all were scrapped by the corporation during December 1938.
D. W. K. Jones Collection/Online Transport Archive

The second major influence in the development of the 'Standard' type came through the Hurst Nelson-built 'Motherwell' open-top bogie cars – Nos 42-53 – that were new in 1902. These were the trams that introduced the 'Tudor Arch' lower-deck windows – familiar on all the 'Standards' – to the Blackpool fleet. All had been equipped with top covers – as shown by No 45 running through floodwater on Central Drive on 1 September 1922 – by 1915. However, wartime exigencies led to their temporary storage from 1915 and, after the war, there was a need to replace them. The bogies of five were used in the rebuilding of the 'Marton Box Cars,

whilst a number were used – for accounting purposes – as notional rebuilds for the 'Standards' of the same number. In reality, little of the original tram was reused – often, as in the case of No 45 (a notional rebuild of 1928), nothing more than the top cover. Of the 12 in the batch, all had effectively been replaced by 'Standards' by 1929 with the exception of No 52; when this was withdrawn in 1932 the production of 'Standards' had ceased and so the withdrawn tram was not directly replaced.

D. W. K. Jones Collection/Online Transport Archive

10

The third type of tram to influence the development of the 'Standards' was represented by the 'De Luxe' four-wheel and bogie cars supplied by the UEC in 1911; one of the latter – No 66 – is seen here at the then new station at Bispham in 1926. The design of the open-balcony top cover, with the two large central windows, plus the use of the Preston McGuire bogies were to be replicated in the 'Standards'. Nos 62-68 were regarded as amongst the most successful of the fleet; had financial circumstances been more propitious, it's likely that Blackpool might have acquired more of the type and that the 'Standard' might never have evolved. The seven trams were all scrapped between 1934 and 1939.

D. W. K. Jones Collection/Online Transport Archive

A busy scene at Gynn Square which, although undated, can be placed between March 1932, when No 34 received its enclosed lower-deck vestibules, and April 1937, when the tramways operated by Lytham St Annes were abandoned. In addition to the 'Standard' and the Lytham car, also visible are one of the 'Dreadnought' type of double-decker and single-deck cars of three generations, two of which are in operation on the route to and from North Station along Dickson Road. No 34 was one of the original quartet of 'Standards' constructed at Rigby Road during 1923 and replaced the 'Marton Box Car' of the same number; never equipped with enclosed balconies, No 34 was destined to be a relatively early casualty, being withdrawn in 1947 and scrapped in October 1951.

D. W. K. Jones Collection/Online Transport Archive

The 'Standards' were equipped with McGuire-type equal-wheel bogies supplied by either Hurst Nelson of Motherwell (Nos 33, 34, 43, 46, 53, 99, 100) or English Electric of Preston. All were eventually equipped with English Electric-built bogies; typical was No 158 as seen in this detailed view taken in August 1952. *Phil Tatt/Online Transport Archive*

TALBOT SQUARE, BLACKPOOL.

A busy scene at Talbot Square in the early 1930s sees passengers boarding 'Standard' No 155 before it heads off along Clifton Street with a service via Marton as an open-balcony car approaches down Talbot Road with a service from Layton. The Layton route was converted to bus operation on 19 October 1936. At the time of writing work is in progress in installing tram track and overhead along the section from Talbot Square along Talbot Road to provide a new tram connection to Blackpool North railway station. *John Meredith Collection/Online Transport Archive*

No 160 was completed at Rigby Road in early September 1927 and was amongst the earliest of the type to be fitted with enclosed lower-deck vestibules. Modified in late 1929, it was one of three to be so treated that year. It is seen here in its original red livery shortly after the modification was completed; the tram was to be repainted into the new green livery in November 1934. *R. Elliott/Courtesy A. D. Packer*

Completed at Rigby Road in February 1929, No 51 – pictured here in 1931 in its original red and white livery – was the penultimate 'Standard' to be completed and was one of only two of the type – the other being No 177 – that was built with the lower-deck vestibules already enclosed. No 51 was constructed reusing the top deck that had previously fitted to Hurst Nelson-built No 51. *Author's Collection*

On 6 April 1949 No 28, seen here at South Promenade picking up passengers prior to heading north to Central station, was used in place of an open 'Boat' during wet weather. Passengers no doubt appreciated the covered accommodation although some intrepid travellers seem to prefer the open balconies. No 28 was new originally in September 1927 and had enclosed lower-deck vestibules fitted in June 1930. In 1940 the tram received a replacement lower-deck vestibule, following accident damage, from withdrawn No 46. The tram was one of those withdrawn as a result of the introduction of the 'Coronation' type; it was taken out of service during 1951 and was scrapped in April 1958.
John Meredith/Online Transport Archive

The dubious honour of being the first 'Standard' to be withdrawn belongs to No 33, seen here at Central Pier, which was taken out of service by the middle of July 1940 and scrapped the following month in Blundell Street. The reasons for withdrawal are uncertain, but a major fault would seem to be indicated. The trucks and motors were retained and used as a 'float' thereafter, the latter being first reused under No 153. No 33 had originally been constructed at Rigby Road in September 1923 when it was fitted with Hurst Nelson maximum-traction bogies; these were replaced in March 1927 by Preston McGuire equal-wheel bogies. In August 1930, the tram received enclosed lower-deck vestibules along with replacement motors and controllers.
Geoffrey Morant Collection/Online Transport Archive

The first 'Standards' to be constructed at Rigby Road were the four completed during the autumn of 1923. The second of this quartet was No 34; it is pictured here at the Talbot Square terminus. Although the photograph is undated, it must have been taken between January 1931, when it was fitted with enclosed lower-deck vestibules (it received modified lower-deck seating at the same time), and October 1933, when it was fitted with deeper rocker panels and was repainted into the new green livery. The tram still carries the destination 'Victoria Pier'; this was the original name of Central Pier until it was renamed in 1930. No 34 was withdrawn in September 1947 following an accident; the following month its bogies and motors were transferred to No 100 although it was not until October 1951 that the remains of the tram were finally scrapped in Blundell Street depot. *Maurice O'Connor/National Tramway Museum*

It may be the summer but, judging from the coats and the eagerness with which the passengers are boarding No 35 en route to Central station on 15 August 1950, the weather seems unseasonable. No 35 was the penultimate 'Standard' built at Rigby Road in 1927 and entered service on 5 October that year. It was fitted with lower-deck platform vestibules during March 1932 and, in October 1934, emerged in the new green livery. One of the 'Standards' to be withdrawn in late 1952, No 35 was scrapped in Blundell Street during December 1953.
A. D. Packer

With the entrance to North Pier in the background, two of the open-balcony 'Standards' await departure from the Talbot Square terminus. History had, however, differing fates for the two cars; whilst No 40 on the right was to survive to become the last open-balcony four-wheel tram to remain in service, No 36 was withdrawn in 1952 and scrapped two years later. The latter tram was new in 1925 and was fitted with lower-deck vestibules in April 1931 before being repainted in the new green and cream livery during October 1934. On 14 April 1944 No 36 was involved in an accident when it derailed at the junction of Abingdon Street and Church Street and ran into a shop. The recovery of the tram required the removal of the canopy at the damaged end which was repaired before the tram re-entered service.
W. J. Wyse

A contrast in front ends at Talbot Square on 13 June 1949. On the left is No 37; this was completed at Rigby Road in October 1927 and modified with enclosed lower-deck vestibules in October 1931. No 39, which was built at Rigby Road in July 1926, was rebuilt as fully enclosed in April 1930 when both the vestibules and balconies received attention; it was one of the earliest to receive this treatment (the other car converted as early was No 159). No 37 carries its destination indicator in its original position; No 39 shows it relocated above the windscreen of the lower-deck vestibule. The fully-enclosed 'Standards' were inconsistent in the location of the destination indicators. In December 1949 No 39 was experimentally fitted with the English Electric bogies salvaged from 'Sun Saloon' No 16 following the latter's conversion to VAMBAC operation; this experiment was not a success. Of the two, No 39 was the earlier to be withdrawn – in 1950 (being scrapped in September 1951) – whilst No 37 succumbed in 1952 and was scrapped in December 1953.
Julian Thompson/Online Transport Archive

The last 'Standard' to be built at Rigby Road during 1926 was No 38, which entered service in November that year. In June 1930, the car was rebuilt as fully enclosed; it underwent a further modification during June 1933, when it was fitted with deeper rocker panels and was repainted into the new green livery. On 20 October 1934, No 38 was involved in an accident with No 66 that resulted in the latter being scrapped. The damage to No 38, which included the underframe being twisted, resulted in the tram's body being lifted to facilitate repair. Although No 38 survived, it was destined to be a relatively early casualty, being taken out of service in January 1945. Its trucks were then transferred to No 149; thereafter No 38 remained in store until being scrapped in October 1951 in Blundell Street depot.
Maurice O'Connor/National Tramway Museum

Destined to be the last of the open-balcony 'Standards' to remain in service and to operate the last passenger service from Talbot Square to Marton when the route was converted on 28 October 1962, No 40 is pictured here at Talbot Square prior to heading towards Royal Oak on 9 September 1948. In the background one of the next generation of double-deck cars can be seen heading southbound along the Promenade route. No 40 was new in February 1926 and was equipped with lower-deck vestibules in December 1931. Withdrawn following the conversion of the Marton route (but officially on 12 January 1963) when it was the last service car from Talbot Square to Marton depot, No 40 was preserved and passed to the Tramway Museum Society to be based at Crich.

Michael H. Waller/Courtesy A. D. Packer

When the Light Railway Transport League annual convention for 1955 was held in Blackpool, the opportunity was taken to inspect Southampton No 45, which was the first electric tram to be privately preserved when purchased in 1948. With no dedicated tramway museum until the purchase of the site at Crich in the late 1950s, No 45 was stored at a number of locations – including Marton depot on Blackpool – and it is pictured here behind 'Standard' No 41. After its time in Blackpool, No 45 was to move to Beaulieu in 1958 before a final move to Derbyshire. No 41 was new originally in 1925 and was to become fully enclosed in May 1932. It remained in service until it was taken out of service following an incident in 1959 when it split the points; officially withdrawn in 1960, it was scrapped in March the following year.

F. K. Farrell/Online Transport Archive

Completed at Rigby Road in May 1926, No 42 – which is seen here outside Marton depot in August 1952 – was one of those that was constructed using one of the top covers reused from one of the older 'Motherwell' cars. It received enclosed lower-deck vestibules in February 1930 and was to become fully enclosed in July 1938 – the last to be completed before the outbreak of World War 2. No 42 was to remain in service until 1953 (when withdrawn following an accident), being scrapped in April 1958.
Phil Tatt/Online Transport Archive

Pictured in front of the Clifton Hotel is No 43; this was the prototype of the 'Standard' type and was completed in Blundell Street works during 1922 and 1923. Incorporating a new underframe and lower deck, the tram incorporated the top cover previously fitted to 'Motherwell' No 43. Initially equipped with Hurst Nelson bogies, these were replaced in November 1924 by Preston McGuire equal-wheel bogies. It was fitted with lower-deck enclosed vestibules in June 1933 and repainted in the new green livery at the same time. Four years later, in April 1937, the lower deck seating was modified. No 43 was withdrawn during 1951 and was scrapped in Blundell Street during October 1952.
D. W. K. Jones Collection/Online Transport Archive

No 45 is pictured at the Royal Oak terminus as the driver carefully eases the tram over the crossover and as the trolleypole inches its way along the reverser. No 45 was new originally during 1928 and was constructed at Rigby Road using the top cover salvaged from the 1902 Hurst Nelson-built car of the same number. It was rebuilt with enclosed lower-deck vestibules in March 1935 and was repainted into the new green and cream livery at the same time. Following an accident, it was withdrawn in late 1951 and was scrapped in Blundell Street depot during February 1954.
Geoffrey Morant

Standing in late October 1950 at the South Pier terminus of the seasonal service to North station via Marton is No 48. New in February 1928, No 48 received lower-deck vestibules September 1931 and was to emerge as fully enclosed in February 1938. One of three of the type to be withdrawn in 1962, No 48, which had operated the last service from Royal Oak to Marton on 28 October 1962, was secured for preservation by the Oregon Electric Railway Historical Society in the United States and sailed from Hull on board the *Sibonga* in August 1964. It reached Portland on 25 September 1964 and remains based with the OERHS.
Peter N. Williams/Online Transport Archive

No 49 was one of the notional rebuilds of an earlier car by the corporation in Rigby Road and as such incorporated the top cover with rounded ends that had been carried by the earlier No 49. In reality, however, No 49, seen here turning from Talbot Square onto the Promenade, was a new tram, equipped with new Preston McGuire equal-wheel bogies, underframe and lower deck. It received enclosed lower-deck vestibules in April 1930 and, exactly three years later, was to be fitted with deeper rocker panels; it was repainted into the new green livery at the same time. A further four years elapsed before a further modification – this time to the lower-deck seating – was undertaken before the tram was converted to fully enclosed in March 1938. One of the type to survive the 1950s, No 49 was withdrawn following the conversion of the Marton route in October 1962. Preserved by the Tramway Museum Society the tram was transferred to Crich two months later. A regular performer at the Museum, the tram last operated in 1992 but remains on display.
Mervyn Robertson Collection/Online Transport Archive

On 17 April 1949 No 51 has completed the run along the residential Marton route and has arrived at the Royal Oak terminus. In the background is the triangular junction with Lytham Road. In the summer months, some Marton cars turned south onto Lytham Road in order to reach the South Pier and provide direct access to the Promenade and nearby beach. In January 1941 No 51 was to receive replacement bogies and motors salvaged from No 46, which had been withdrawn and scrapped the previous year. Surprisingly, given that it was amongst the newest built, No 51 was never to receive enclosed balconies and was to become a relatively early casualty. It was withdrawn during 1952 as a result of the introduction of the VAMBAC-fitted trams to the Marton service and scrapped in June 1954.

Michael H. Waller/Courtesy A. D. Packer

New in March 1923 as one of the two pre-production 'Standards' (alongside No 46), No 53 – pictured here on 21 August 1936 – was built in Blundell Street utilising the Hurst Nelson bogies, which were replaced by Preston McGuire equal-wheel equivalents in February 1928, and blunt-ended top cover salvaged from 'Motherwell' car No 53 on new underframes and lower deck. The car was equipped with enclosed lower-deck vestibules in August 1931 and was repainted into the new green livery in July 1934; the prominent 'Blackpool Corporation' visible on the side panels between the two decks was discontinued in 1940 (presumably as a wartime measure initially but not reinstated after the war). The lower deck seating was also amended in July 1934. Withdrawn in 1950, No 53 was scrapped in Blundell Street in October 1952. Following the tram's demise, its bogies and motors were transferred to No 41.

Mervyn Robertson Collection/Online Transport Archive

Looking in good external condition at Royal Oak in August 1951, No 99 was approaching its final year in service. Withdrawn in September the following year, No 99 was dismantled in Blundell Street during late 1954. The tram had originally been constructed at Rigby Road in late 1923 when it was equipped with Hurst Nelson maximum traction bogies; these were replaced with Preston McGuire equal-wheel bogies during October 1925. The car was fitted with enclosed lower-deck vestibules in September 1931 and had its lower-deck seating altered at the same time. Repainted in the green livery during November 1934, the tram underwent a major body overhaul during May 1936.
Phil Tatt/Online Transport Archive

Pictured in front of Martin depot are 'Standard' No 100 and 'Pantograph' No 174 (on a tour). The latter was one of a batch of 10 – Nos 167-76 – supplied by English Electric that were – as the name suggests – originally fitted with pantographs, but these were replaced by conventional trolleypoles during 1933 and 1934. The batch was initially fitted with McGuire equal-wheel bogies also supplied by English Electric but these were replaced during 1950 by bogies reused from 'Sun Saloons' Nos 10-21 when the latter were converted to VAMBAC operation. No 174 was last used in passenger service in October 1959 and was used, having lost its motors, as the basis of the Santa Fe trailer illuminated car in 1962.

No 100 was one of four 'Standards' completed in Rigby Road during 1923. In June 1926 its original Hurst Nelson maximum traction bogies were replaced with Preston McGuire equal wheel bogies and, in February 1930, it was rebuilt as fully enclosed. As such, it became the first 'Standard' to have enclosed top-deck vestibules. At the same time its lower deck seating was modified. In October 1947 it received replacement bogies and motors – reused from No 34 (which had been withdrawn the previous month as a result of accident damage) – before being withdrawn in September 1952. It was finally to be dismantled in Blundell Street during November 1954. *R. F. Mack*

One of six of the type to be completed at Rigby Road during 1924, No 143 was to be rebuilt with enclosed lower-deck vestibules in December 1929 and as fully enclosed in February 1932. One of three to be withdrawn during 1957, it was to escape the attentions of the scrap merchants and was to emerge in July the following year rebuilt into a new works car (see page 60). *W. S. Eades/Online Transport Archive*

Recorded at Pleasure Beach during August 1952 is No 144; this tram was completed at Rigby Road during 1925 and received enclosed lower-deck vestibules in February 1930. Destined to be one of a number of the type withdrawn during 1952, No 144, which succumbed during October that year, was the first 'Standard' to be preserved when it was sold to the Seashore Trolley Museum at Kennebunkport in Maine. On 11 March 1955 it became the first Blackpool tram to cross the Atlantic when it departed from Liverpool Docks on board the United States Line freighter *American Press* bound for Boston en route to its new home where it arrived on 2 April 1955. Used for a number of years as an operational car at Seashore, it was withdrawn with wiring problems. After almost 50 years out of service, work commenced some five years ago on its restoration to operational condition. *Phil Tatt/Online Transport Archive*

The last passenger has just boarded No 145 as it pauses across the road from Marton depot with an inbound working towards Talbot Square on 17 April 1949. The 'Standards' were traditionally associated with the 'Town' routes and the Marton service, until the route saw the introduction of the VAMBAC-equipped cars from 1949 onwards, was one of the key services that they operated. The introduction of the single-deckers to the route led to the withdrawal of a significant number of 'Standards' in the early 1950s including No 145. New from Rigby Road in 1925 and equipped with lower-deck vestibules in January 1935 – the last to be so treated – No 145 was to survive in service until October 1952 and was finally scrapped in April 1958.
John Meredith/Online Transport Archive

On 20 April 1938 – No 160 was rebuilt as fully-enclosed in March 1940 – Nos 146 and 160 pass on Abingdon Street at its junction with Church Street alongside the local branch of the Yorkshire Penny Bank. Since the view was taken the bank has been rebuilt and is now a branch of the Yorkshire Bank whilst both Abingdon Street and Church Street have been pedestrianised at this point. No 146 was the first of the quartet of 'Standards' built by Hurst Nelson in 1924. Fitted with lower-deck enclosed vestibules during the first half of 1932, No 146 was repainted in the new green livery in April 1935. Following the demise of No 50 in December 1940, No 146 received a lower-deck vestibule from the scrapped tram in January 1941. Withdrawn during the late summer of 1950, No 146 was scrapped in Blundell Street during August 1952.
H. B. Priestley/National Tramway Museum

Pictured in late October 1950 at the South Pier terminus on Station Road is No 147; this was the second of the batch of four trams ordered from Hurst Nelson in 1923 and delivered the following year. Fitted with lower-deck enclosed vestibules in June 1933 and fully-enclosed in May 1940 – one of the last four to be so treated – No 147 was to survive to be one of only four 'Standards' to survive in service beyond 1962. Although the first of this quartet to be withdrawn, accident damage to two of the 'Balloons' – Nos 245 and 259 – resulted in No 147 being restored to service in 1965; it and No 160 were the last Blackpool trams to operate with swivel-headed trolleypoles. The remainder of the fleet were equipped with fixed heads for which the overhead along the surviving route was designed to operate. No 147 was again withdrawn on 11 April 1966 but was restored to service on 19 July 1966. Final withdrawal came later in the year when Nos 147 and 159 operated a farewell enthusiasts' tour for the type. Fortunately, No 147 was preserved and it departed on 9 September 1967 on board the *Manchester Commerce* as it made its way to its new home at the Columbia Park Museum in Ohio, USA. No 147 was subsequently repatriated to the UK and is now based again in Blackpool.

Peter N. Williams/Online Transport Archive

No 148 was the third of the four Hurst Nelson-built 'Standards' delivered during 1924. Each of these cost £1,750 – the equivalent at 2020 prices of just over £107,000. The tram was fitted with enclosed lower-deck vestibules in March 1931 whilst, exactly three years later, it was further modified with deeper rocker panels being added; it was repainted into the new green livery at the same time. Withdrawn in October 1951, it was scrapped in Blundell street depot during July 1954. *A. D. Packer*

Looking in superb external condition when recorded here at Royal Oak during August 1951, No 149 was, despite appearances, one of the batch to be withdrawn the following year. New originally in 1924 as one of the quartet ordered from Hurst Nelson in 1923, the tram had received lower-deck vestibules in April 1932 and, in August 1940, was rebuilt as fully enclosed – the last 'Standard' to undergo this modification. Spending some two years in store after withdrawal, No 149, which was one of the 'Standards' fitted with the destination blinds set at a lower level, was one of those scrapped during October 1954. *Phil Tatt/Online Transport Archive*

Recorded in front of Marton depot on 17 April 1949 is No 150. New in 1925 as one of those constructed by Hurst Nelson, No 150 gained lower-deck vestibules in October 1931 but was amongst the last of those to become fully enclosed, with work on this not being completed until May 1940. No 150 was amongst those 'Standards' withdrawn in 1951 but was not scrapped until three years later. Marton depot originally dated to 1901 but was extended towards the rear in 1912. It closed as an operational tram depot on 28 October 1962 but was used for a period thereafter for the scrapping of redundant trams; the track and overhead to the depot were last used on 11 March 1963 when three trams – including 'Standard' No 48 – left the depot for the last time heading to Rigby Road via Talbot Square. The depot was eventually sold and demolished with a filling station later being constructed on the site.

John Meredith/Online Transport Archive

A wartime view – as evinced by the shielded headlamp and the white painted collision fender (both designed to deal with issues relating to the overnight blackout) – taken on 13 October 1940 sees No 151 on Whitegate Drive, Marton, on an outbound service towards Royal Oak. No 151 was one of three 'Standards' completed by Hurst Nelson that entered service, alongside Nos 150 and 152 during December 1925. It was to receive enclosed lower-deck vestibules in November 1930. One of the type to receive deeper rocker panels – again as clearly shown in this view – with this modification being completed in June 1933; the tram was repainted into the new green livery at the same time. Withdrawn in late 1952, No 151 was one of the type scrapped in Blundell Street during October 1954.

Mervyn Robertson Collection/Online Transport Archive

The last of three constructed by Hurst Nelson during the year, No 152 – seen here at Royal Oak in 1950 – was also the last of the 'Standards' to enter service during 1925 – on 18 December – and was to receive enclosed lower-deck vestibules in July 1930. No 152 was the last tram to operate to Layton on 19 October 1936 when the trams were replaced by motorbus. Taken out of service finally in late 1952, No 152 was scrapped six years later.
C. Carter

One of the crew seems to be in a slightly quizzical mood as he examines the rear of No 153. New in May 1926, No 153 was to receive enclosed lower-deck vestibules in January 1929 – the first of the type to receive this modification – although it was never to be rebuilt as fully enclosed. The arrival of the Roberts-built 'Coronation' class resulted in the withdrawal of five of the surviving 'Standards' – including No 153 – in 1954. The tram was to be scrapped in 1958. *F. E. J. Ward/Online Transport Archive*

Standing at the South Pier terminus on 17 April 1949 prior to heading into town via Marton to Talbot Square is No 154. New in June 1926, No 154 received enclosed lower-deck vestibules in February 1930 – one of the first to be so treated. No 154 was the last service car on the Layton route when the service was converted on 19 October 1936. Withdrawn in December 1950, No 154 was finally scrapped in September 1952. *Michael H. Waller/Courtesy A. D. Packer*

As passengers board No 145 in Talbot Square prior to departure towards Royal Oak, No 155 is arriving at the terminus with its destination display already altered for its next outbound trip. New in July 1926, one of six 'Standards' built by the corporation that year, No 155 was rebuilt in August 1930 as fully-enclosed. No 155 was also one of the type to be fitted with deeper rocker panels – in September 1933 – as is evident in this view which shows No 145 with its standard rocker panels. No 155 was withdrawn in the later summer of 1952 and scrapped in Blundell Street during November 1954. *C. Carter*

As one of the streamlined 'Railcoaches' makes its way northwards in August 1952. Standing on the centre road at Central Station, the crew of 156 are preparing the car for its return journey. It would be one of many 'shorts' which, during the season, served the busiest section of the Promenade. This third track enabled through cars to pass on either side. Although looking clean and smart, No 156 was withdrawn at the end of the 1952 season. New in May 1927 and given enclosed lower-deck vestibules in October 1933, In 1940 the tram received a replacement lower-deck vestibule, following accident damage, from withdrawn No 46. No 156 was scrapped in April 1954.

Phil Tatt/Online Transport Archive

Fully-laden No 158 is seen here at Royal Oak about to leave for Talbot Square in August 1951. The car had emerged from Rigby Road in June 1927. In June 1930 it was equipped with lower-deck vestibules and was to become fully enclosed six months later. No 158 was one of two 'Standards' to be selected in 1959 to become illuminated cars to replace the existing – and life-expired – trams used for that purpose. Note the high position of the destination indicator; not all of those 'Standards' converted to fully enclosed saw the destination indicator raised to this level. *Phil Tatt/Online Transport Archive*

Nos 158 and 159 entered service a day apart in June 1927 – the former on the 8th and latter on the 9th – and the two led almost parallel lives for almost 40 years. No 159 received fully enclosed lower-deck vestibules in February 1930 and its upper-deck balconies were enclosed at the same time, resulting in it becoming the first fully-enclosed 'Standard', whilst No 158 became fully enclosed by the end of the same year. This view records the pair in the late 1950s before both became illuminated cars in August 1959. No 159 was used on 28 October 1962 to convey the final passengers – the official group – from Talbot Square to Marton depot. Both it and No 158 remained operational until the end of October 1966; thereafter their paths diverged. No 159 was secured for preservation at the East Anglian Transport Museum at Carlton Colville and first operated there in November 1970. Whilst No 158 was secured by the Tramway Museum Society and transferred to Crich, its fate was to be dismantled for spares and its remains were finally scrapped in May 1978.

M. J. Lea/LRTA (London Area) Collection/Online Transport Archive

Delivered in September 1927 No 160 – pictured here inside Marton depot on 7 September 1962 – was amongst the earliest to be rebuilt with enclosed lower-deck vestibules – in September 1929 – but ironically was amongst the last to be rebuilt as fully enclosed. The work was undertaken in March 1940, one of four to receive enclosed balconies that year. Pictured alongside the 'Standard' are the two of open toastrack cars – Nos 165 and 166 – that were rebuilt for use by television crews during the illumination season in 1953 and 1956 respectively. Following final withdrawal, No 166 was preserved and restored to its original condition at Crich in the early 1970s. No 160, one of the quartet of the type to survive in service post-1962, was less fortunate; finally withdrawn on 11 April 1966, the car was to sacrifice its motors at the end of June the same year for use in works car No 752. The remains of No 160 were scrapped in Blundell Street depot during April 1967. *L. Collings/Online Transport Archive*

As members of the crew chat alongside No 28, the last of the passengers disembark from No 177 at the Talbot Square terminus. In theory No 51 ought to have been the last of the 'Standards' constructed; in the event, however, sufficient parts remained at Rigby Road for the construction of one final car – No 177 – which was completed in July 1929. Like No 51, No 177 was completed with lower-deck vestibules enclosed and was to be subsequently rebuilt as fully enclosed. No 177 was withdrawn in 1952 and scrapped in April the following year.
Michael H. Waller/Courtesy A. D. Packer

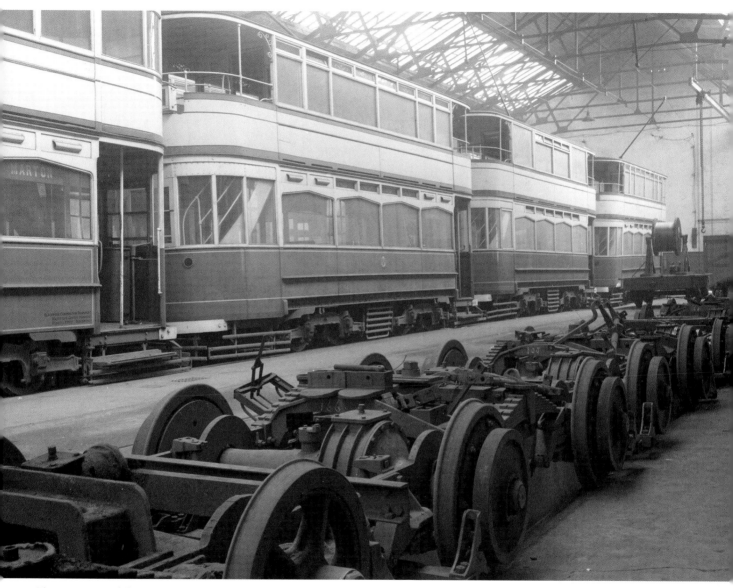

The conversion of the Marton route to operation by the VAMBAC-equipped single-decks cars between 1949 and 1951 resulted in a significant number of 'Standards' being withdrawn. In all, between 1949 and 1951, no fewer than 10 of the type were withdrawn from service. Pictured awaiting their fate in Blundell Street depot – with fully-enclosed No 150 on the extreme left – are four of the withdrawn trams. All were finally scrapped between October 1951 and December 1954. *R. W. A. Jones/Online Transport Archive*

With one of the original 1898 crossbench cars of the Blackpool & Fleetwood Tramroad Co in the middle also awaiting its fate, work is in hand during June 1952 on the dismantling of a number of redundant 'Standards' in Blundell Street depot. A total of 10 of the crossbench cars were delivered for the opening of the line to Fleetwood on 14 July 1898; built by G. F. Milnes, the 10 became

Nos 126-35 when the corporation took over the route on 1 January 1920. A number were to be used for works duties after withdrawal and one of the batch – No 127 (ex- Blackpool & Fleetwood No 2) – was restored for the system's 75th anniversary in 1960 after spending some years in use as a snowplough.
G. F. Ashwell/Online Transport Archive

One of those undergoing scrapping at this time was No 142; the photographer was present to witness the vehicle being turned onto its side to facilitate the work. With the dismantling gang standing in front of the tram, this was to be the sad fate of the tram after more than a quarter century of service. Blundell Street was the original depot of the Blackpool Electric Tramways Co and opened in 1885; rebuilt in 1898 it acted as the corporation's workshops until the new Rigby Road Works opened in 1922. The expansion of the latter to include a running shed resulted in Blundell Street being relegated to a store and location to dismantle redundant trams. It was finally to be demolished in 1982. *G. F. Ashwell/Online Transport Archive*

No 145 is pictured again but for a final time as the withdrawn tram – along with five other 'Standards' – awaits its ultimate fate at Thornton Gate. Withdrawn during 1956, No 145 was finally scrapped in April 1958.

R. L. Wilson Collection/Online Transport Archive

By the late 1950s the corporation's existing fleet of illuminated cars was increasingly aged and the decision was taken to replace them. Thus, during 1959, two of the remaining 'Standards' – Nos 158 and 159 – were modified with lighting and other decorative features. One of the duo is pictured here on the approach track to Rigby Road depot with the coach station – a familiar destination for generations of holidaymakers and enthusiasts – in the background. *F. E. J. Ward/Online Transport Archive*

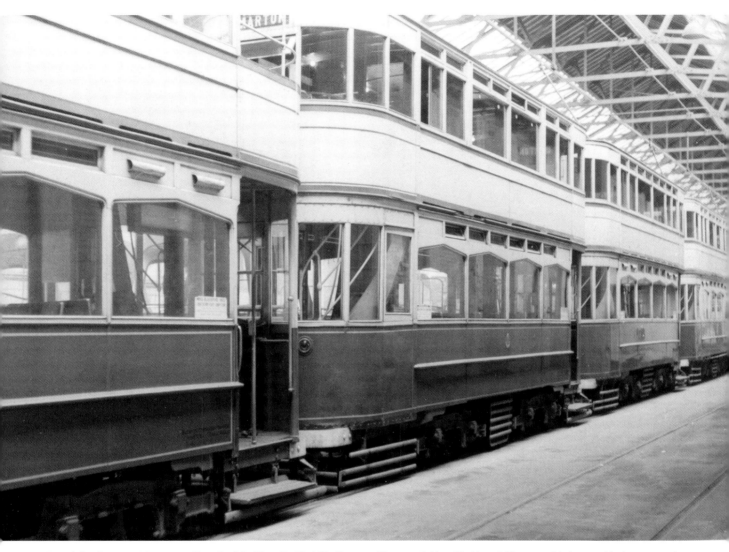

Five of the then surviving seven 'Standards' – Nos 40, 48, 147, 49 and 160 – are recorded inside Marton depot on 7 September 1962. The other two survivors – Nos 158 and 159 – had, by this date, been converted into illuminated cars. Of the quintet illustrated, Nos 40, 48 and 49 were withdrawn with the conversion of the Marton route and all three were to be preserved; Nos 147 and 160 both lasted until 1966 with No 147 eventually being preserved in the USA. *Les Collings/Online Transport Archive*

Following its withdrawal, converted 'Marton Box Car' No 31 was transferred to the Engineering Department in 1934. In order to accommodate an overhead inspection platform (in order to be able to work on sections of the promenade route inaccessible to road-based tower wagons), the recently renewed top deck cover was removed and the lower-deck vestibules enclosed. Renumbered 4 in the works fleet, the tram is pictured outside Rigby Road depot. No 4 was renumbered 754 in 1972 and remained in use until withdrawn in April 1983. Subsequently preserved, the tram was restored to the open-top condition as it existed in the early 1920s similar to that shown by No 30 on page 8. Based at the museum since its restoration, the tram returned briefly to Blackpool during 1998 and 1999 as part of the celebrations for the centenary of the Fleetwood route.
F. E. J. Ward/Online Transport Archive

One of the 'Standards' withdrawn in the late 1950s was No 143; unlike most of those withdrawn at the time, No 143 evaded the attention of the scrap merchants and was to emerge in July 1958 converted into an additional works car. With its top cover again removed to facilitate the installation of an inspection platform, the tram was also equipped with an 8.6 litre diesel engine – reused from a redundant Leyland TD5 – in order to enable it to continue operating when the overhead was switched off. Renumbered 753, it is pictured here at the loop at Bispham. The tram remained in use until 1990 when, following a fire, it was withdrawn. Although scrapping seemed its likely fate, it was eventually preserved by the Lancashire Transport Trust. It returned to Blackpool in 2013 and has subsequently been restored to its original condition with open balconies and lower-deck vestibules. Now based at Rigby Road for use on heritage tours, the restored tram was relaunched officially on 23 September 2019. *J. Joyce/Online Transport Archive*

Over the years a number of Blackpool trams have made the crossing of the Atlantic; in certain cases on several occasions. The first tram, however, to make the trip was 'Standard' No 144. Stored after withdrawal in September 1952, it was secured for preservation by the Seashore Trolley Museum of Kennebunkport, having been donated to the museum by the Mayor and Aldermen of Blackpool. Shipped on the freighter *American Press* it arrived at its new home in Maine on 2 April 1955. The tram is seen here shortly after its arrival in the USA still in the green and cream livery in which it last operated in Blackpool. The tram was subsequently restored to the red and cream livery that it wore pre-World War 2. Out of service from the late 1960s, work started to restore the vehicle to operational condition in 2017. Now operational again and restored to its green and cream livery, No 144 is the only one of the four British trams owned by the museum – the others being Glasgow 'Coronation' No 1274, Leeds 'Feltham' No 526 and Liverpool 'Baby Grand' No 293 – that is in service at the museum.
Frank Hunt/LRTA (London Area) Collection/Online Transport Archive

Although both of the 'Standards' modified in the late 1950s to act as illuminated cars – Nos 158 and 159 – were sold after withdrawal, No 158, which passed to the Tramway Museum Society and left Blackpool for the last time on 5 May 1967, was destined to be used for spares and it was finally dismantled in 1978. No 159, however, had a happier fate; sold to the East Anglian Transport Museum, it departed from Blackpool on 17 April 1967 bound for its new home at Carlton Colville. Restored to its pre-illuminated condition, No 159 is pictured at the museum on 7 August 1976. *R. L. Wilson/Online Transport Archive*

The fate of No 158 was not as rosy as that of No 159. Withdrawn in October 1966, the tram was sold to the Tramway Museum at Crich and transported there in May 1967. With the museum already owning two 'Standards', No 158 was acquired as a source of spare parts and was finally scrapped in May 1978. The tram is seen here looking in a very poor condition as it awaits its ultimate fate.
Mervyn Robertson Collection/Online Transport Archive

In 1985 Blackpool celebrated the centenary of its electric tramway and, to mark the event, a number of historic Blackpool trams – plus those from a number of other tramways in the British Isles – were loaned to the corporation to mark the anniversary. Amongst those that made a nostalgic return to the coast was No 40 from the National Tramway Museum, which is recorded here in Fleetwood on 16 June 1985 restored, following an overhaul during 1983 and 1984, to the red and cream livery that it wore prior to repainting in green and cream in September 1934.
R. L. Wilson/Online Transport Archive